A Rare
NATIVITY

Sam Beeson

IMAGES BY Nina & Terral Cochran

ENSIGN
PEAK

For those I have
hurt or offended.

Forgive me.

—SAM

Text © 2015 Sam Beeson
Illustrations © 2015 Studio III, LLC

Visit us at EnsignPeakPublishing.com

Library of Congress Cataloging-in-Publication Data

Beeson, Sam, author.
  Rare nativity / Sam Beeson ; images by Nina and Terral Cochran.
     pages cm
  Includes bibliographical references.
  ISBN 978-1-62972-062-3 (hardbound : alk. paper)
1. Créches (Nativity scenes)—Poetry. 2. Christmas poetry. I. Cochran, Nina, illustrator.
II. Cochran, Terral, illustrator. III. Title.
  PS3602.E367R37 2015
  811'.6—dc23   2015004717

Printed in China
RR Donnelley, Shenzhen, China

10 9 8 7 6 5 4 3 2 1

Ye have heard that it hath been said, Thou shalt love thy neighbour, and hate thine enemy. But I say unto you, Love your enemies, bless them that curse you, do good to them that hate you, and pray for them which despitefully use you, and persecute you.

—Matthew 5:43–44

On the first night of Christmas I gave my enemy
a briar from a tanglewood tree.

On the second night of Christmas I gave my enemy
two broken eggs.

On the third night of Christmas I gave my enemy
three crooked forks.

On the fourth night of Christmas I gave my enemy

four old potatoes.

On the fifth night of Christmas I gave my enemy
five shards of glass.

On the sixth night of Christmas I gave my enemy
six crumpled tissues.

On the seventh night of Christmas I gave my enemy
seven scraps of paper.

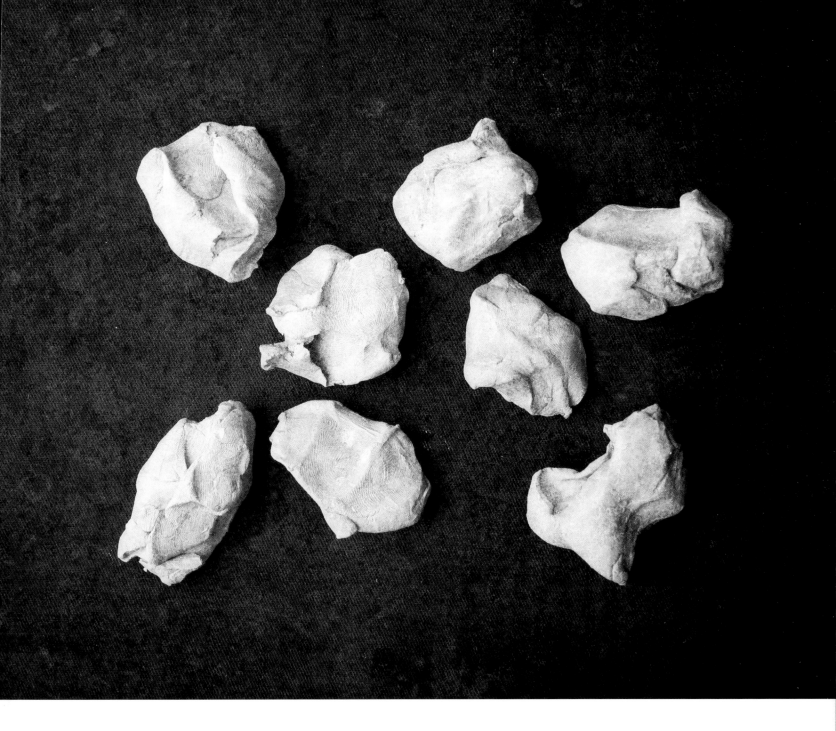

On the eighth night of Christmas I gave my enemy
eight clumps of clay.

On the ninth night of Christmas I gave my enemy
nine rusty nails.

On the tenth night of Christmas I gave my enemy
a bird nest in ten pieces.

On the eleventh night of Christmas I gave my enemy
eleven dead leaves.

On the twelfth night of Christmas I gave my enemy
twelve gnarly twigs.

The night that followed number twelve,
                    I slept 'til half past three.

And wallowed in my sallow state
                    Against my enemy.

I dreamed my enemy convulsed.
I dreamed he gagged and swore.
My dreams were dashed as I awoke
To knocking at the door.

I grumbled out of bed and then
I shuffled toward the sound.
I opened up the door to find
A gift upon the ground.

The tag upon the lid contained
A note addressed to me.
I recognized the penmanship.
It was my enemy:

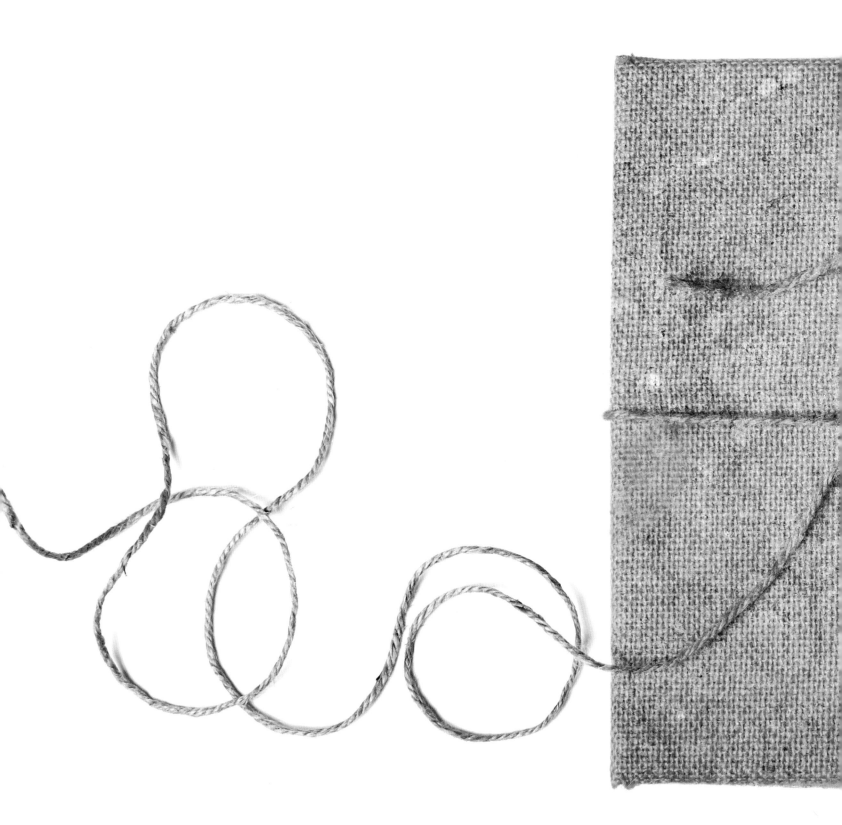

I gently pulled the knotted twine,
And setting it aside,

I lifted up the lid
    To the compendium inside.

Five shards of glass composed a star—
A singular display.

And sheep were made of tissue.
Bits of bird nest made the hay.

Potato shepherds came to life
With carvings and with clays.

As paper angels shouted out
Their wonders and their praise.

Three kingly forks each bowed a head
Near rusted, spiky pegs.
The briar baby lay between
The pale, parental eggs.

All foolish things, all rotten things
I'd sent my enemy,
Were carefully converted in
This rare nativity.

He turned the other cheek and made
My ugliness a gem.
And by so doing, pointed me . . .

. . . to lovely Bethlehem.